WE ARE BEEKEEPERS

By: Fatima D. El-Mekki

Photos by: Sharif and Fatima D. El-Mekki

Hello friends,

My name is Zaynab, and I am seven years old. My birthday is on February 15th. My favorite color is mint green. My favorite book is *Zoey and Sassafras* by Asia Citro. When I grow up, I want to be the first black woman president of the United States. If somebody else becomes it before me, I want to do something amazing for my people.

My name is Zakiyyah, I am Zaynab's little sister. I am six years old, and my birthday is on October 20th. My favorite colors are white and green. My favorite book is *Elephant and Piggy* by Mo Willems. I do not know what I want to be when I grow up yet, but I still have plenty of time to decide.

We don't know exactly what we will do in the future, but we know what we are currently doing!

We are beekeepers!

Many people wonder what beekeepers are and what they do.

"Zakiyyah, can you answer the question?"

"A beekeeper is someone who keeps bees."

"Thanks, Zakiyyah! That is a great answer."

Throughout this book, we will give you even more details about honeybees, beekeepers, and **apiaries**.

We were quite young when our older brother, Saleem, started his apiary and became a beekeeper. The first time we brought honeybees home, we were curious and a little nervous at the same time; curious because we did not know that we could maintain bees in our backyard and nervous because we knew that bees could sting. We were also nervous because we went with our father and our brother to a farm to pick up the bees. At the time, we did not realize we would need to ride back home – a seventy-four-mile trip – with a box of honeybees! The box allowed us to bring the honeybees safely to their new home, an apiary, in our backyard.

In this picture, we were looking at the box of honeybees we would share a car ride home with. It took us over an hour to get home. Now, can you understand why we were a little apprehensive? But we made it home without incident. Whew!

Would you want to take a ride with a box of seven to ten thousand bees?

Our dad gifted us with beekeeper suits as Eid gifts (Eid is an Islamic holiday celebrated after the last day of the holy month of Ramadhan). We were so happy to be able to help our brother and father with our family's apiary! Dad told us that wearing our suits will prevent us from being stung by bees. We felt very safe when we wore them. They were snug, cool, and comfortable.

Our beekeeper suits have three parts: a round veil, a bodysuit, and gloves. We must make sure that our socks are long enough to tuck the bottom of our pants into It, so the bees will not find a way to get into our suits.

We think we look like little astronauts. What do you think?

A beekeeper is someone who keeps honeybees in a beehive, like the one you see. This is one of our beehives, and you can see bees flying around. There are different types of beehives. Our brother prefers the Langstroth model. Do you wonder why there is a rock on top of it? It makes it harder for animals such as racoon, skunks, or even a strong wind from opening the top of the hive. A single hive can have between 20,000-80,000 honeybees. These hives will likely have a couple hundred drones (male bees), only one queen, and all the rest are the queen honeybee's daughters!

There are a lot of frames inside the beehive; their foundations are made up of a lot of cells made of beeswax, all exactly alike. There is a lot of math in a honeybee hive. What shape do you think honeycombs are?

Do you see Zakiyyah holding a frame of comb, larvae, and honeybees?

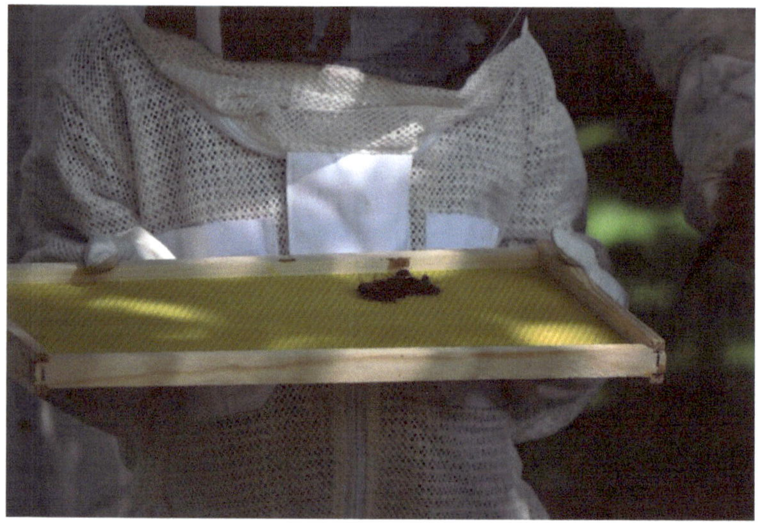

This frame is a new foundation. As you can see, there are not a lot of bees on it. They have not started putting wax on the frame yet. I wonder what the honeybees are communicating to each other.

You can tell that this is not a new frame. The covered cells in this frame are protecting the **brood**; each covered cell has a larva that is preparing to transform into honeybee just like their sisters and brothers. When the larvae (brood) are ready and fully formed, they eat their way out of the covered cells. Most will be daughters of the queen honeybee, and some will be her sons (drones).

Honeybees build wax cells called honeycomb; it has six sides and has the shape of a hexagon. Honeycomb cells are used to store the food (nectar, pollen, beebread, or honey) or eggs and larvae.

It takes a whole lot of bees and a whole lot of work for a hive of bees to fill all the comb with nectar, pollen, and honey. The queen bee lays eggs in empty cells and the worker honeybees place honey or pollen in empty cells too. It is like a race – each cell is either for food or for the queen's eggs.

Depending on the size, a frame can hold between 4,600-8,400 cells.

Sometimes it is not easy to take the frame out of the beehive because the honeybees make a substance from tree sap called propolis to seal all the cracks throughout the hive. It is as strong as glue. Some people say it is great medicine, but we have not used it, yet. Because it is so sticky, we need to use a hive tool like the one our dad is holding in the picture, to open the hive and separate the frames from each other.

Before our dad takes a frame out of the beehive, we need a device called a *smoker* like the one I am holding. We fill it with pine needles and our dad lights it with a lighter. The smoke helps to calm the bees and disrupts their communication, so they will not sting us. These bees are constantly communicating with each other. They use chemicals and dances to communicate their needs and where a great patch of flowers is. If they think they are being attacked, they can communicate with each other with chemicals that alerts for danger. Guard bees and others will try to protect their honey and their home. The smoke from the smoker makes them think there might be a fire and therefore, they will start eating honey in case they must abandon their hive and take their honey with them. It does not harm the honeybees and it's very important not to use too much.

When we conduct a hive inspection, we check for the queen, the larvae, the eggs, the pests such as mites, hive beetles, wax moths and the amount of honey the honeybees have produced. We want to make sure the apiary is healthy, and we move slowly so we do not alarm the bees. If we are calm, they are more likely to remain calm.

Let's review what we know about bees now.

The eggs look like grains of rice at first and as they grow, they go through their developmental cycle or their four stages of metamorphosis, from egg to larva, to pupa and, at the end a fully formed honeybee.
It takes three days for an egg to hatch and 21 days to become an adult bee. In this picture, the eggs look like grains of rice and the worm-looking shape next to the eggs are larvae.

The bees are separated in 3 categories: the **queen**, the **drones**, and the **foragers**.

The **queen** bee is much longer and larger than the other honeybees. Her job is just to lay eggs. That is her only job, and she fully understands her assignment! A queen can live up to five years and the other bees take full care of her – even feeding her. She lays one thousand or two thousand eggs in little cradles of wax in one day if she is healthy.

In this picture, the queen has a turquoise dot on her back. Sometimes beekeepers make small, harmless marks on the queen to make it easier to find them when inspecting the beehive.

Pay close attention to the picture, you will see that the queen is larger than the others. Do you see all the capped brood?

The males in the hive are called **drones**. They have large black eyes. Their job is to help the queen get pregnant and have babies. The drones cannot sting. They are larger, fatter than the females, but not as long as a queen. Drones do not collect nectar or pollen and they do not build cells or feed the larvae. In fact, they do not do much of anything. They eat and wait to see if a queen nearby needs to mate. In the winter, the other honeybees kick them out of the hive, so they do not eat all their stored food.

The **foragers** (worker honeybees) are the ones you will see flying from one flower to another. They are all girls, daughters of the queen. Foragers will visit many flowers and trees, sometimes up to two miles in a single trip, collecting nectar, pollen, tree sap, and water to drink. They store the nectar in their honey stomach, a special bag in their tummies, until they can return to the hive and pass it into the mouth of another bee. It goes from that bee to another and another. This process makes the nectar lose water, it becomes stickier and helps them make honey.

A honeybee foraging for nectar or pollen might visit between 50-100 flowers during a single trip. She often returns to their hive carrying almost half of her weight in pollen and nectar. Can you imagine running (or flying) carrying half of your weight? Honeybees from a hive must visit approximately two million flowers and fly fifty-five thousand miles to make a single pound of honey. A single hive (or colony) of honeybees can produce between sixty and hundred pounds of honey each year! That is a lot of flying, collecting, and producing! No wonder people sometimes describe a super productive person as *busy as a bee*.

Every time a forager goes from one flower to another it moves pollen from one flower to the next. This action is called pollination. This helps the fruits, nuts, or seeds on trees to be healthy as possible. Honeybees are great pollinators. Many crops would suffer if honeybees did not exist.

The foragers clean inside the hives, care for larvae, build cells, store honey, take care of the queen, pollinate, guard the nest, and feed drones. They are busy bees!

Female honeybees have four phases in their lives before dying:

1. They go to work immediately after they hatch from the egg and clean the cell from where they emerge.

2. They feed young brood. This role lasts for a week.

3. They move away from the center of the hive and build honeycomb, store food, and guard the nest. This role lasts about a week.

4. In the last phase, they become foragers, leaving the colony to find pollen, and feed the colony. They work until they die. If a bee dies inside the hive, it is taken out by other bees. They have a life expectancy of about three weeks if they are born in summer, much longer if they are born in the winter.

Do you have any idea why the honeybees make honey?

During the warm seasons, the honeybees get their food from pollen or nectar. When the cold seasons arrive, there are less and less flowers and the only food they can eat is the honey they stored. So, they make honey to eat during the cold season. Aren't they smart?!

Since I am talking about seasons, I want to tell you something amazing about the honey! Because the nectar and pollen that the honeybees collect during the spring, summer, and fall seasons are different, the honey also has assorted colors and tastes!! The lighter colored honey is from the spring season and the darker colored honey is from the fall season. When you look at the picture of the assorted colored honey, the one on the far left has honey that has crystalized, it means the honey became hard. Sometimes we make toast and add butter and crystalized honey for a snack. Absolutely delicious!

We hope you get to try it one day, if you haven't already!

Can you tell which jar contains the honey we harvested in the fall?

Although, honeybees must travel far and wide, we planted different flowers to support our lovely pollinators. Our grandfather and uncle helped us plant various kinds of flowers in our backyard so that the honeybees and other pollinators have a variety. They like that.

Sometimes, the honeybees leave the colony and the hive for various reasons. It can be because the conditions in the hive are not comfortable anymore, or they do not feel secure, or there are just too many honeybees inside of their hive – they can get crowded too. When the honeybees leave the hive, they form a cluster because they are homeless and need to find a new place. This migration is called a swarm and it can contain thousands of honeybees.

In this picture, the honeybees swarmed on a very tall tree in our backyard. Our father had to call his friend to bring a taller ladder to help him get them back to the hive. Swarming happens to most apiaries and this kind of situation is well known by beekeepers.

How do we get honey, you might ask? After checking the frames inside the hives, we put it in a special spinning machine that extracts the honey from the frames.

When we get a lot of honey, or a surplus, we share it with our family, friends, and neighbors. Our older sister, Sakinah, who is a young entrepreneur, sells the extra honey that we have left. She puts it in different containers as you can see in the picture.

Do you want to become a beekeeper and do not know where to start? You can attend a honey fest in your city to learn more.

Ask the beekeepers questions and taste honey like we do sometimes.

Hopefully, our experiences have taught you something new. We are beekeepers because we love nature, honeybees, and honey. We also help honeybees (and other pollinators) because without them, our world's food supply might be negatively impacted. One third of our food is pollinated by honeybees. We need them more than they need us.

Let's end with some fun facts!

1. Bees are the only insects that make food that human beings can eat.

2. Honey never rots - even after many years. They have found edible honey in mummy tombs, or sarcophaguses.

3. Honeybees have 5 eyes, three small ones on top of their head and two big ones in front.

4. Honeybees communicate by dancing and through smell. They use pheromones, which are chemicals that they can smell.

5. The queen can choose to lay female eggs or male eggs, depending on what she senses the hive needs.

6. Bees can die when they sting. Their stinger is barbed (has a hook on it so it can stick in the skin of whatever it stung). While this barbed stinger can get out of the skin of an insect that it might sting, human skin is thick, and it is hard for the stinger to come out. So, when the bee tries to pull herself out, she ends up tearing up her abdomen and dies.

When a honeybee stings, she leaves behind the venom sac in the human skin. The stinger stays in the skin, pumping its venom into your body, causing pain, and swelling, and worse if you are allergic to bee venom. Our father was stung once without his suit, he removed the venom sac to decrease the amount of venom in his body. He is fine, by the way.

7. The foragers have a distinct way to communicate between them, it is called bee dance. The honeybees shake their abdomen all around to communicate with other honeybees where to find flowers.

8. Did you know honey is like a bee's vomit? That makes me and my sister giggle every time we eat some. There is no other throw up I can imagine eating!

9. Have you ever heard a flying insect like a bee? Honeybees make a loud buzzing sound when they are flying around. The sound comes from their wings, which beat two hundred times per second. That is a lot of flapping!

Thanks for reading! If you enjoyed this book about bees, perhaps next time, we will share some information about our chickens with you.

www.ingramcontent.com/pod-product-compliance
Lightning Source LLC
Chambersburg PA
CBHW040320240726
48664CB00006B/1573